21 Days of Prayer + Fasting 2025

Spirit-*Filled* Prayer

What's Inside

The manifestation of the Spirit

A people of His presence

Direction, protection and revelation

Empowered and sent

Let's join together in Spirit-filled prayer

Foursquare President Randy Remington encourages us to pray with "structure, commitment and accountability."

Spirit-filled prayer is the engine that powers the church and its mission. It is the key that unlocks the power of God. Consider this exhortation from the apostle Paul:

"And pray in the Spirit on all occasions with all kinds of prayers and requests. With this in mind, be alert and always keep on praying for all the Lord's people" (Eph. 6:18, NIV).

Paul offers practical guidance for Spirit-filled prayer:

- **Pray in the Spirit.** God's Spirit is an active participant in prayer.
- **Do it on all occasions.** There is always time to pray.
- **Include all kinds of prayer.** Employ intercession, petitions, praises, confession and the use of Scripture.
- **Remain alert and consistent**, focusing your prayers on God's people.

I believe with all my heart that if we devote ourselves to Spirit-filled prayer, we will see God move in mighty ways.

The kind of prayer Paul commands in Ephesians 6:18 requires structure, commitment and accountability. Let's embrace that together. Let's intentionally give ourselves to Spirit-filled prayer that we might also "be strong in the Lord and in His mighty power" (Eph. 6:10).

I am grateful to be praying with you!

Randy Remington

Randy Remington
President
The U.S. Foursquare Church

Prayer + fasting resources

Dive deeper with further reading and family enrichment during 21 Days of Prayer + Fasting 2025.

How does the Holy Spirit help us pray?

As we enter this new year with prayer and fasting, it's a good time to remind ourselves that we are not alone in our intercession. We have a Helper who has been sent by the Father to strengthen us in many ways, but none is more important than our ability to pray effectively.

Read the full article by Foursquare Pastor Steve Schell to learn about three of the ways that the Holy Spirit helps us pray. Find the article at **Foursquare.Church/HolySpiritPrayer**.

Why do we fast?

There are many reasons to fast and a variety of methods to practice this important spiritual discipline. Read the full article by Foursquare Pastor Bill Gross to learn more about why this discipline is important and what the Bible says about fasting, as well as the practicalities of how to fast. Read it at **Foursquare.Church/Fasting-2025.**

Don't forget to pause for Family Moments

Make 21 Days of Prayer + Fasting a family affair. Download the Family Moments book with daily activities, or purchase a full-color version on Amazon. Head to **FoursquarePrayer.org** for details on this year's Family Moments, available in both English and Spanish.

More prayer + fasting resources

Want to dive into prayer, fasting and the gifts of the Holy Spirit, but you aren't sure where to start? Find even more helpful resources on prayer, fasting and the Holy Spirit, including resources for kids, at **FoursquarePrayer.org**.

También disponible en español

¡Descargue o compre una copia de los 21 Días de Ayuna + Oración 2025 en español! Inscríbase para recibir correos electrónicos y encuentre recursos para la iglesia también. Visite **OracionCuadrangular.org**.

The inward work *of the* Spirit

08

When we confess Jesus Christ as Lord,
the Spirit of God brings the life of Jesus
into us, and us into the life of Jesus.
From the moment of our salvation,
the Holy Spirit begins a lifelong work
within us, leading us to deny the works
of our sinful nature, enabling us to live
as a new creation and testifying to our
identity as children of God.

09

Renewed by the Spirit

What can God's grace and mercy, given freely and unearned by us, do in our lives?

Today's Scripture

"He saved us, not because of righteous things we had done, but because of His mercy. He saved us through the washing of rebirth and renewal by the Holy Spirit, whom He poured out on us generously through Jesus Christ our Savior."
—Titus 3:5-6 (NIV)

"Therefore, I want you to know that no one who is speaking by the Spirit of God says, 'Jesus be cursed,' and no one can say, 'Jesus is Lord,' except by the Holy Spirit."
—1 Corinthians 12:3 (NIV)

Reflect on the Word

In a letter filled with ethical advice and calls to good works, Paul emphasizes that our good deeds are not a way to earn God's favor, but a response to the grace we've already received in Jesus Christ (Titus 3:5). We have already received God's grace through His incredible mercy, given to us freely. Yes, we are called to live disciplined, purified and spiritually committed lives—not to get closer to God, but because we want our own lives to reflect our new identity in Him.

Paul also refers to the "washing" work of the Spirit, a reminder that through baptism, God has cleansed us by His Spirit. We don't do good to earn this cleansing, or His favor; we live out our faith as a grateful response to Him for saving and redeeming us.

Prayer + Contemplation

01 ——— Reflect on the grace and mercy you have received through Jesus Christ. How has this unearned favor given you a new identity in Him? How does this mercy motivate you to live your life in response to this?

02 ——— Ask the Holy Spirit for the strength and guidance to help you live a disciplined and spiritually committed life, embodying the grace and mercy you have been shown.

03 ——— Lift up those who are struggling to understand the concept of God's grace. Pray that they may come to know the joy and freedom of living as recipients of God's unearned favor.

Notes + Reflection

Day — 02
Made alive
in Christ

How does Jesus' resurrection manifest in our own lives, and how can we allow ourselves to be transformed by it?

Today's Scripture

"You, however, are not in the realm of the flesh but are in the realm of the Spirit, if indeed the Spirit of God lives in you ... And if the Spirit of Him who raised Jesus from the dead is living in you, He who raised Christ from the dead will also give life to your mortal bodies because of His Spirit who lives in you."
—Romans 8:9,11 (NIV)

"The thief does not come except to steal, and to kill, and to destroy. I have come that they may have life, and that they may have it more abundantly."
—John 10:10 (NKJV)

"I have been crucified with Christ and I no longer live, but Christ lives in me. The life I now live in the body, I live by faith in the Son of God, who loved me and gave Himself for me."
—Galatians 2:20 (NIV)

Reflect on the Word

The resurrection is the most significant event in the life of Jesus and it also has a huge impact on our own lives.

The passage from Romans tells us that the same Spirit who raised Jesus from the dead now lives in us, bringing new life to our "mortal bodies" (v. 11). This is not just a future hope but a present reality. The resurrection power of the Holy Spirit transforms us from a life bound by sin and death to one filled with purpose and vitality in Christ.

Paul emphasized this truth to help us grasp the profound miracle of resurrection, urging us to understand that the same power that raised Christ is at work within us. Through the Spirit, we are raised to a new life, filled with hope, purpose and the promise of eternal life.

Prayer + Contemplation

01 ———— Reflect on the incredible truth that the same Spirit who raised Jesus from the dead now lives in you, giving you new life and purpose in Christ.

02 ———— Ask the Holy Spirit to guide you to live fully and abundantly in Christ, to give you a deeper understanding of this resurrection power in your daily life.

03 ———— Lift up those in your life who feel spiritually dead or disconnected, praying that they may experience the life-giving presence of the Holy Spirit and be made alive in Christ.

Notes + Reflection

_____

_____

_____

_____

Day — 03
Beloved children of God

By the Holy Spirit we are made sons and daughters of God, and may enjoy a close relationship with Him as Heavenly Father.

Today's Scripture

"The Spirit you received does not make you slaves, so that you live in fear again; rather, the Spirit you received brought about your adoption to sonship. And by Him we cry, 'Abba, Father.'"
—Romans 8:15 (NIV)

"Because you are His sons, God sent the Spirit of His Son into our hearts, the Spirit who calls out, 'Abba, Father.'"
— Galatians 4:6 (NIV)

"And hope does not put us to shame, because God's love has been poured out into our hearts through the Holy Spirit, who has been given to us."
— Romans 5:5 (NIV)

Reflect on the Word

Jesus addresses God as "Abba", a Hebrew word for "father." This term does not mean a formal, distant relationship but rather a close, intimate relationship with a profound level of affection and trust.

This same intimate relationship is offered to us through the Holy Spirit, as explained in Romans 8:15. The Spirit in us makes us sons and daughters of God, granting us the privilege to call Him "Abba." This adoption causes a total transformation of identity, allowing us to experience security as God's beloved children.

Prayer + Contemplation

01 ——————— Take time to address God as "Abba, Father" intimately. How does doing this transform your view of God's love and of your identity as His child?

02 ——————— Ask God to help you live confidently under His love and protection. Pray for a deeper experience of the Holy Spirit as you embrace your new identity as God's beloved child.

03 ——————— Pray for those in your life who are distant from God to experience His love and the security of being His children, finding peace and joy in His embrace.

Notes + Reflection

_____

_____

_____

_____

_____

_____

_____

Life *in the* Spirit

Being filled with the Holy Spirit is not primarily a formula, a doctrine or a mystical experience. It's the condition of a person who intends to be a disciple. There is more to Christianity than believing the right things; there is Someone to receive and experience.

Day — 04
Praise and thanksgiving

Let's consider the myriad things in our lives for which we should be thankful to the Lord.

Today's Scripture

"Rejoice always, pray without ceasing, in everything give thanks; for this is the will of God in Christ Jesus for you. Do not quench the Spirit."
—1 Thessalonians 5:16-19 (NKJV)

"And do not be drunk with wine, in which is dissipation; but be filled with the Spirit, speaking to one another in psalms and hymns and spiritual songs, singing and making melody in your heart to the Lord, giving thanks always for all things to God the Father in the name of our Lord Jesus Christ, submitting to one another in the fear of God."
—Ephesians 5:18-21 (NKJV)

Reflect on the Word

Not everything in the Bible is easy to understand, but there are passages of Scripture that are quite clear. The passage in 1 Thessalonians says we must:

- **Rejoice always.** Start by identifying some of the thieves of your joy, such as guilt, grief, grudges and grumbling. Decide to approach life from an opposite spirit. Choose joy instead.
- **Pray continually.** Prayer doesn't have to be flashy. As a matter of fact, it's best if it isn't. Just talk to God, and let Him talk to you. In your relationship with the Lord, make sure to listen as much, if not more, than you speak.

- **Give thanks.** The apostle Paul begins 10 of his 13 New Testament epistles with some expression of gratitude. His prayers and letters were peppered with thanks, despite the ongoing challenges he faced. One could say Paul's letters are "thank full!" We are invited to be the same, by giving thanks

Prayer + Contemplation

01 ——————— You may have had many valid reasons to grumble and complain in the past few years, and yet God's will for our lives is to rejoice, pray and give thanks. How will that shape your response to Him in the future?

02 ——————— Take a moment to pray to the Lord with gratitude. Keep it simple. Say thank you to Him for what He's given you. Listen to His heart.

03 ——————— Make a list of what you are grateful for today. That list may prompt a phone call, text or note to people who have had a positive impact on your life.

Notes + Reflection

_____

_____

_____

_____

Day — 05

Repentance and forgiveness

It isn't enough to simply be forgiven, though it is essential; we must also repent and turn in a new direction with God's help.

Today's Scripture

"Let no corrupt word proceed out of your mouth, but what is good for necessary edification, that it may impart grace to the hearers. And do not grieve the Holy Spirit of God, by whom you were sealed for the day of redemption. Let all bitterness, wrath, anger, clamor and evil speaking be put away from you, with all malice. And be kind to one another, tenderhearted, forgiving one another, even as God in Christ forgave you."
—Ephesians 4:29-32 (NKJV)

Additional Scripture

—John 16:7-11 (NKJV)

Reflect on the Word

The story is told of a critical person who approached Methodism founder John Wesley at a church service, saying, "My talent is to speak my mind." Wesley allegedly replied: "That's one talent that the Lord would not care a bit if you buried!"

Humorous as it is, there is nothing funny about the unwholesome and unconstructive talk that so often comes out of our mouths. We are exhorted to get rid of bitterness, rage, anger, brawling, slander and malice. That's a good start; however, it doesn't end there.

We must then replace it with that which is much better: kindness, compassion, forgiveness and love. This transformative process is a work of the Spirit. Our appropriate response to the work of the Spirit is repentance, and the bearing of spiritual fruit in keeping with that repentance.

Prayer + Contemplation

01 ———— Reflect on these scriptures and allow the Holy Spirit to come alongside you, helping you get rid of that which ought not to be in your heart, and replace it with something much better.

02 ———— When approaching challenging situations, pray Psalm 141:3 over your life: "Set a guard over my mouth, O Lord; keep watch over the door of my lips" (NKJV).

03 ———— Have you been speaking your mind in an unwholesome way, whether to a person's face, behind their back or online? We can't undo the past, but we can repent of it. Take a moment to repent, seeking forgiveness from the Lord and, perhaps, even from any particular person you've offended.

Notes + Reflection

_____

_____

_____

_____

_____

_____

_____

Day — 06
Truth and freedom

In these uncertain times, we must lean on the Spirit of the Lord to discern truth and be obedient.

Today's Scripture

"Then Jesus said to those Jews who believed Him, 'If you abide in my word, you are my disciples indeed. And you shall know the truth, and the truth shall make you free ... Therefore if the Son makes you free, you shall be free indeed.'"
—John 8:31-32,36 (NKJV)

"Now the Lord is the Spirit; and where the Spirit of the Lord is, there is liberty."
—2 Corinthians 3:17 (NKJV)

"However, when He, the Spirit of truth, has come, He will guide you into all truth ..."
—John 16:13 (NKJV)

Reflect on the Word

In the study of leadership theory, a concept called "VUCA" has emerged that reflects the culture of our times. VUCA stands for Volatility, Uncertainty, Complexity and Ambiguity.

There's no question that we are living in a VUCA world right now, with so many things that are hard to understand or fully know. But there are some things we can know.

We can know if we are a disciple of Jesus. How? Jesus told those who believed in Him, "If you continue to obey my teaching, you are truly my followers" (John 8:31, NCV). One of the primary marks of a disciple of Jesus is obedience to the Word of God. It's been said that

Christians are generally educated far beyond their level of obedience. This means we know a lot, but unfortunately we do not always show this with our actions. Do not delay to obey Him, especially in these times of volatility, uncertainty, complexity and ambiguity.

Prayer + Contemplation

01 —————— Are you a follower of Jesus who is walking in freedom, and in the Spirit of truth? If so, what areas of greater obedience might Jesus be calling you to?

02 —————— Are you yet to become a follower of Jesus? If so, take a moment to pray, asking the Holy Spirit to guide you into all Truth, to Jesus. Ask Jesus to be your Lord and Savior.

03 —————— Prayerfully ask the Holy Spirit to give you more opportunities to obey the leading of the Lord.

Notes + Reflection

_____

_____

_____

_____

_____

_____

The transforming work *of the* Spirit

God's desire for us is that we "be conformed to the image of His Son" (Rom. 8:29, NKJV). His plan for you and me is to make us more like Jesus. How does He do this? That is the work of the Spirit. A genuine encounter with the Holy Spirit sanctifies us, empowers us to grow in Christ's character and enables us to do Christ's work.

Spirit-sourced transformation

God's holy presence has a weight and brilliance, and no one can be in His presence without experiencing profound change.

Today's Scripture

"But we all, with unveiled face, beholding as in a mirror the glory of the Lord, are being transformed into the same image from glory to glory, just as by the Spirit of the Lord."
—2 Corinthians 3:18 (NKJV)

Reflect on the Word

In the passage from 2 Corinthians, Paul refers to Moses beholding the glory of God in the cleft of the rock (Exodus 33). What must it be like to be covered by the hand of God? To feel the weight of His presence in the flesh?

Experiencing this changed Moses—it transformed him irrevocably. We know this because Scripture tells us his face shone, terrifying people (Exodus 34:29-35). Moses covered his face when he wasn't in the Lord's presence.

Because of Jesus' sacrifice, we are able to stand directly at the source, before the weight and glory of God, and don't have to be afraid or ashamed. We don't have to cover ourselves. Because of Jesus, the glory of God shining in us will never fade away. In His presence, we are transformed more and more into the likeness of our beautiful Lord Jesus, by the power of the Holy Spirit.

Prayer + Contemplation

01 ——————— Take a moment to acknowledge the weight of the glory of God as you rest in His presence. Let it transform you into the beloved image of His Son.

02 ——————— Ask God to increase your intimacy with Jesus, that your desire for Him and the things of Him would grow.

03 ——————— Pray that churches would long to be transformed by His all-consuming presence, that the Spirit of God would baptize in fire, melting away fear and anything that doesn't look or sound like Jesus.

Notes + Reflection

_____

_____

_____

_____

_____

_____

_____

_____

Day — 08
Spirit-governed thoughts

Our thoughts create our world, but how are those thoughts formed, and what do we allow to influence them?

Today's Scripture

"This is what we speak, not in words taught us by human wisdom but in words taught by the Spirit, explaining spiritual realities with Spirit-taught words. The person without the Spirit does not accept the things that come from the Spirit of God but considers them foolishness, and cannot understand them because they are discerned only through the Spirit. The person with the Spirit makes judgments about all things, but such a person is not subject to merely human judgments, for, 'Who has known the mind of the Lord so as to instruct Him?' But we have the mind of Christ."
—1 Corinthians 2:13-16 (NIV)

Additional Scripture

—Romans 8:5-6 (NIV)

Reflect on the Word

We tend to focus a lot on how we and others act, but do we take time to determine the source of what leads to our actions? Over what parts of us have we ceded control?

In the passage from Romans, we see a contrast of being governed by the carnal mind, the flesh, or being governed by wisdom, the Spirit of God.

One is focused on self, and the other is focused on God. One leads to death; the other leads to life and peace. One rejects that which is true. The other accepts that we need instruction.

Praise be to the Lord that we have been given an undeserved gift that reveals the secrets of heaven through the mind of Christ! We have the greatest Professor the universe has and will ever know.

Prayer + Contemplation

01 ——————— Take a moment to ask the Spirit to evaluate your heart. What do your actions reveal about who is in control? Who is governing your life: you or the Holy Spirit?

02 ——————— Pray that the Spirit will give you the strength and humility to lay down control and surrender to the mind of Christ.

03 ——————— Pray against the division in our world, country and churches. Ask the Spirit for an outpouring of love and wisdom that will guide us into unity and compassion.

Notes + Reflection

_____

_____

_____

_____

_____

Day — 09
Spirit-formed character and creativity

Just as gold must be refined by fire to be strong and valuable, so must our hearts be refined by holy fire.

Today's Scripture

"Then the Lord said to Moses, 'See, I have chosen Bezalel son of Uri, the son of Hur, of the tribe of Judah, and I have filled him with the Spirit of God, with wisdom, with understanding, with knowledge and with all kinds of skills—to make artistic designs for work in gold, silver and bronze, to cut and set stones, to work in wood, and to engage in all kinds of crafts.'"
—Exodus 31:1-5 (NIV)

"But the fruit of the Spirit is love, joy, peace, patience, kindness, goodness, faithfulness, gentleness, self-control; against such things there is no law."
  —Galatians 5:22-23 (ESV)

Reflect on the Word

Goldsmithing is a fascinating craft. Beautiful jewelry, exquisite coins, breathtaking architecture—they all point back to a maker.

When you see gold in its raw state, you may wonder how it makes such a radical transformation. At first it is rough and unrefined, full of impurities. The addition of fire causes it to make a metamorphosis to smooth and intricate, full of value.

What a beautiful illustration by the Master Craftsman. God Himself is the All-Consuming Fire, and His Spirit is the one who baptizes with fire, melting away the stony, sinful impurities in our hearts, so that we become soft and pliable in His hands. And after all that is insignificant is consumed and separated, what remains is our character, the fruit of His labor and the work of His hands. Revival fire starts in us.

Prayer + Contemplation

01 ———— Take time to reflect on the beauty and wisdom of the Master Craftsman. To know that we are crafted in His image, endowed with gifts and baptized in fire so that we can show the world His glory. Do our lives reflect the beauty of our Maker? Are there places in our hearts that need to be consumed by the fire of His presence?

02 ———— Pray for a spirit of repentance in the church, that we would plead for the Lord to search our hearts and surrender to the fire of His presence that melts away anything that doesn't look like Him.

03 ———— Pray for a fresh baptism of fire; for the Spirit to fill us with His gifts; and for love and compassion for the lost.

Notes + Reflection

The Manifestation
of the Spirit

To separate the gospel message from its supernatural origin and power is to diminish it. God wants to take us from spiritual infancy into the maturity of Spirit-empowered service. After all, His goal for each generation is to save as many as possible and to build His church, revealing His grace and glory. To that end, He uses Spirit-led and Spirit-empowered people.

Day — 10
Praying in the Spirit

When we use God's gifts to speak to Him, we're able to pray about things we don't yet comprehend with our own understanding.

Today's Scripture

"Likewise the Spirit also helps in our weaknesses. For we do not know what we should pray for as we ought, but the Spirit Himself makes intercession for us with groanings which cannot be uttered. Now He who searches the hearts knows what the mind of the Spirit is, because He makes intercession for the saints according to the will of God."
—Romans 8:26-27 (NKJV)

Additional Scripture

—Jude 20-21 (NIV)
—1 Corinthians 14:2 (NIV)

Reflect on the Word

Most of life is spiritual, comprising things we can't grasp with our physical senses and mysteries we can't fathom with natural thinking. Good intentions and masterful plans don't really make much progress against spiritual forces. That's why we pray.

But when we don't know what God wants to do in our situation, or when we can't find words to adequately express what's in our heart, how do we pray? Thankfully, we're not left on our own to figure out what to pray. The Holy Spirit offers to lead us.

The Spirit knows what's in God's heart and exactly what He wants in our life. He directs our intercession accordingly, leading us to pray about spiritual mysteries and God's will for our life.

The Spirit may also put words on our lips to express sentiments that are beyond our understanding. Because God's thoughts aren't like ours, Spirit-led prayer words don't make sense to our minds. Our "mother tongue" enables prayer for what we do understand, and our "other" tongue allows us to pray about what we don't.

Prayer + Contemplation

01 ———— The Lord knows the circumstances in your life right now, as well as what's behind them. What is the benefit of praying in the Spirit?

02 ———— What is something big you've been praying about using your own understanding? Would you consider praying about it with the Spirit (1 Cor. 14:15)?

03 ———— Paul spoke in tongues more than his contemporaries did (1 Cor. 14:18). This week, will you take time to pray in the Spirit more than you usually do?

Notes + Reflection

_____

_____

_____

_____

Day — 11
Spiritual gifts

The gifts of God are not mere personality traits, but Holy Spirit manifestation of His glory working through us.

Today's Scripture

"There are diversities of gifts, but the same Spirit. There are differences of ministries, but the same Lord. And there are diversities of activities, but it is the same God who works all in all. But the manifestation of the Spirit is given to each one for the profit of all: for to one is given the word of wisdom through the Spirit, to another the word of knowledge through the same Spirit, to another faith by the same Spirit, to another gifts of healings by the same Spirit, to another the working of miracles, to another prophecy, to another discerning of spirits, to another different kinds of tongues, to another the interpretation of tongues. But one and the same Spirit works all these things, distributing to each one individually as He wills."
—1 Corinthians 12:4-11 (NKJV)

Additional Scripture

—Romans 12:6-8 (NIV)

Reflect on the Word

Every daughter and son of God, each member of Christ's body, has been given spiritual enabling that grants us access to understanding and power beyond our own. These gifts are not personality traits or talents; they can't be found in anyone's toolbox. Instead, they come from above.

Though generally referred to as "spiritual gifts," these capacities to function supernaturally include more than one category of spirituals (gifts and ministries) and different ways in which they work (activities). For instance, the gift of prophecy isn't the same as the ministry of a prophet, and some prophecies console while others announce the future.

Over time we grow more sensitive to the Spirit's prompting to exercise a gift and function in our ministry. And we learn to cooperate more fully with the Holy Spirit, speaking words He gives us to share and taking actions He bids us do.

Prayer + Contemplation

01 ——— Re-read today's scripture passages aloud, and ask God to give you insight about your spiritual giftedness.

02 ——— This week, how will you make space to minister with your unique spiritual gifts?

03 ——— Pray that you and your church will operate more fully with the spiritual tools and capacities He has

Digital resource

Watch this video from Daniel A. Brown, Ph.D., to learn more about the gifts of the Holy Spirit. **Foursquare.Church/Gifts-2025**

Notes + Reflection

_____

_____

_____

_____

Miracles

The first steps to miraculous deliverance are Spirit-guided prayer and faith in the works of Jesus.

Today's Scripture

"How God anointed Jesus of Nazareth with the Holy Spirit and power, and how he went around doing good and healing all who were under the power of the devil, because God was with him."
—Acts 10:38 (NIV)

"And God confirmed the message by giving signs and wonders and various miracles and gifts of the Holy Spirit whenever He chose."
—Hebrews 2:4 (NLT)

Reflect on the Word

Jesus always demonstrated His kindness and care for the countless broken and hurting. That same love and compassion that flowed from the heart and hands of Jesus continues to cover the earth today. No matter what the need, Jesus is willing and waiting to be involved. He is never too busy running the universe that He won't immediately flood your life with His presence and touch. Anyone who reaches toward heaven will find peace, power and sometimes unexplainable joy, even during some of the greatest trials in life.

People have personally witnessed blind eyes, deaf ears and everything in between being miraculously touched by the power of the Holy Spirit. He is and will always be the God who loves bringing life to His people. Whatever you might be facing, trust that the same Jesus who cared for those hungry, hurting, bound, infirmed and hopeless will be the answer and bring calm to every storm in life.

Prayer + Contemplation

01 ———— Look back through the scriptures and remember how Jesus never failed to show His love and care for any that had need. Remember that "Jesus Christ is the same yesterday and today and forever" (Heb. 13:8, NIV). Jesus is, and always will be, Lord over every situation or circumstance in this life.

02 ———— Pray for your own faith level to rise and believe that Jesus, in the same way as when He walked this earth, will work miracles in your life and the lives of those around you. As a first step, pray as the early believers did when they asked the Lord, "Increase our faith" (Luke 17:5, NKJV).

03 ———— Take a moment today to bring needs before the Lord that seem unfixable. They may be your own, a hurting family member's or a friend's. Begin a journey of believing that the same Jesus who walked above the raging seas can meet you where and when a miracle is needed.

Notes + Reflection

_____

_____

_____

_____

A people
of His presence

21 Days of Prayer + Fasting 2025

The church is called to be the very presence of Jesus in the world. Through the church, God is instilling the world with His life and love. What does the church offer? A physical experience with a transcendent God. The world needs something more significant than religion; they must experience God. Prayer, unity, passionate love for Jesus and a dependence on the Holy Spirit are all hallmarks of a people living out their calling.

Day — 13
A spiritual church

What is a church? Not a building, location or even a meeting, but a "spiritual house" made of "living stones," Scripture says.

Today's Scripture

"You also, like living stones, are being built into a spiritual house to be a holy priesthood, offering spiritual sacrifices acceptable to God through Jesus Christ."
—1 Peter 2:5 (NIV)

"...'Not by might nor by power, but by my Spirit,' says the Lord Almighty."
—Zechariah 4:6 (NIV)

"Yet I hold this against you: You have forsaken the love you had at first. Consider how far you have fallen! Repent and do the things you did at first. If you do not repent, I will come to you and remove your lampstand from its place."
—Revelation 2:4-5 (NIV)

Reflect on the Word

What makes our places of worship sacred? What's so special about gathering in a sanctuary or living room or coffee shop or school cafeteria? Where's the value? Is it the place? Is it the people? The value of our worship gatherings is found in the One whom we gather to worship.

The church is the very presence of Jesus in a people. This means we, the church, are not just a group of people with common beliefs. We don't just meet once a week because we enjoy the same style of preaching or the same worship songs. We are spiritually united by the presence of Jesus in our lives and in our midst when two or three of us gather in His name.

Together, we are "living stones" being built into a spiritual house—a house that is not a sanctuary, coffee shop, living room or cafeteria. In this spiritual house Immanuel, God with us, dwells.

Prayer + Contemplation

01 ———— In 1 Peter 2:5 we are called a holy priesthood offering spiritual sacrifices to God. What spiritual sacrifices do you make to God?

02 ———— Take a moment to consider the gift it is to know and love our Savior. Let's give thanks to Him for being Immanuel, God with us.

03 ———— Pray for the church universal, that it will continue to grow across the globe and that we, its living stones, will continue to be built up.

Notes + Reflection

_____

_____

_____

_____

Day — 14

A bold and courageous church

The world may make us anxious, fearful and timid, but God has called the church to overcome that for His glory.

Today's Scripture

"For the Spirit God gave us does not make us timid, but gives us power, love and self-discipline."
—2 Timothy 1:7 (NIV)

"And when they had prayed, the place where they were assembled together was shaken; and they were all filled with the Holy Spirit, and they spoke the word of God with boldness."
—Acts 4:31 (NKJV)

Reflect on the Word

We all have experienced opportunities to fear. Maybe you've been faced with seemingly impossible situations, and have had to make what feels like impossible decisions. Maybe you've felt paralyzed with fear and anxiety. If not for the matchless blood of Jesus, we'd be stuck in that place: overcome and overwhelmed by fear.

We can be deeply grateful for His Holy Spirit, living in us, giving us power, love and self-control. His gift of self-control is what empowers us to take all those thoughts captive and make them obedient to Christ.

God has not given His people a spirit of fear; He has given us power. And with every test and every trial, we grow in power, our courage is strengthened, and our impact increases.

As His people, we have a vital assignment to boldly shine the light of Jesus. We are called to live empowered lives, emboldened by His Spirit.

A fearful church is an ineffective church. We are meant to be effective. We are made to be courageous.

Prayer + Contemplation

01 —————— In what areas have you experienced the power, love and self-discipline that His Holy Spirit brings?

02 —————— Read or recite 2 Timothy 1:7 aloud. Then make it personal by saying, "The Spirit You gave me does not make me timid, but gives me power, love and self-discipline."

03 —————— Together, let's pray that the gospel of Jesus Christ will continue to spread across the globe through the willingness of His courageous church.

Notes + Reflection

_____

_____

_____

_____

_____

Day — 15

A unified church

Peace is a radical concept in today's world, but the Holy Spirit can unite the church when we love one another and fix our eyes on Jesus.

Today's Scripture

"For He himself is our peace, who has made the two groups one and has destroyed the barrier, the dividing wall of hostility, by setting aside in His flesh the law with its commands and regulations. His purpose was to create in Himself one new humanity out of the two, thus making peace, and in one body to reconcile both of them to God through the cross, by which He put to death their hostility. He came and preached peace to you who were far away and peace to those who were near. For through Him we both have access to the Father by one Spirit."
—Ephesians 2:14-18 (NIV)

Additional Scripture

—Ephesians 4:1-6 (NIV)
—Psalm 133 (NIV)

Reflect on the Word

One of our Foursquare Creed's statements is a concept that our founder, Sister Aimee Semple McPherson, often shared: "In essentials, unity; in non-essentials, liberty; in all things, charity." As a church, we must be united in the essentials. While we make room for and celebrate our diversity, we must also stand firmly on what we know matters most.

John 13:35 tells us the world will know we are Jesus' disciples by our love for one another. How well do we love? How obvious is that love for one another? Do we, as co-laborers in Christ, love out loud? Do we stand together?

We must be intentional. We must be committed. We must make every effort to pursue oneness. A unified church is founded on the hope of Jesus, bound together by love and united in the Holy Spirit through the bond of peace.

Prayer + Contemplation

01 ——— Ephesians 4:3 says we should make every effort to keep the unity of the Spirit. In what ways do you foster unity?

02 ——— As one body, let's pray for the church to grow in unity—not uniformity, but specifically unity of the Spirit.

03 ——— Let's take a moment to consider ways that we can contribute to unity among our community of believers. Ask the Lord to use you as an agent of His peace.

Notes + Reflection

_____

_____

_____

_____

_____

God wants us to stay near our guide, the Holy Spirit, because He knows our future. It doesn't mean the enemy of our soul won't target us or that we won't experience suffering. It does mean that His presence will be constant, that we will have discernment in every situation, and that we will be divinely equipped to face the battles before us.

Direction, protection, _and_ revelation

Day — 16

Praying for guidance and direction

Without the Holy Spirit guiding us on the path God would have us take, we might become lost and wander from our purpose.

Today's Scripture

"For those who are led by the Spirit of God are the children of God."
—Romans 8:14 (NIV)

"Since we live by the Spirit, let us keep in step with the Spirit."
—Galatians 5:25 (NIV)

"Trust in the Lord with all your heart; do not depend on your own understanding. Seek His will in all you do, and He will show you which path to take."
—Proverbs 3:5-6 (NLT)

Additional Scripture

—Acts 16:6 (NIV)

Reflect on the Word

The tallest tree in the world is called Hyperion, a coastal redwood in California measuring more than 380 feet tall. Even before it was closed to hikers, there were no trails or directions to this behemoth, and a permit was required to enter the park where the tree was located.

For a short time, clues were posted online, yet finding it still required wading through a river and up a stream, identifying the correct logjam and climbing up a hillside. To survey the wonder of Hyperion, these tips were essential.

We all need guidance. At times, we find ourselves stuck, struggling to discover something of value. We cannot depend on our own understanding but need the help of someone who knows the way. The Spirit of God goes before us. As we seek His will in everything and trust in Him fully, He will direct and guide us on a path of infinite worth.

Prayer + Contemplation

01 ———— Take time to reflect on the verses for today. Where are you depending on your own understanding for guidance?

02 ———— Write down what your reflection reveals. Repent for any lack of trust in God that might have been revealed. Ask the Holy Spirit to show you God's path for you.

03 ———— Pray for the church around the world to keep in step with the Spirit of God in order to make Jesus known.

Notes + Reflection

Day — 17

Praying for covering and protection

Be strong and courageous, and put on the armor of God, for spiritual battles we cannot see are being fought all around us.

Today's Scripture

"Finally, be strong in the Lord and in His mighty power. Put on the full armor of God, so that you can take your stand against the devil's schemes. For our struggle is not against flesh and blood, but against the rulers, against the authorities, against the powers of this dark world and against the spiritual forces of evil in the heavenly realms."
—Ephesians 6:10-12 (NIV)

"My prayer is not that you take them out of the world but that you protect them from the evil one."
—John 17:15 (NIV)

Reflect on the Word

There are times in life when following God's direction is like stepping on a hornet's nest with hell's fury seemingly awakened. In John 17:15, Jesus prayed for His church to be protected from the evil one. We can take great comfort that He knows exactly what we're up against and is interceding before the Father on our behalf.

Let the passage from Ephesians 6 become your battle cry as you stand against the enemy's schemes. It requires intention to keep your mind secure in your salvation, to surrender to His righteousness and truth as protection for your life. Let your faith become your shield, and the Word of God be your weapon of warfare.

When you acknowledge your battle is not against the flesh, which readily presents as your enemy, but rather against spiritual forces you cannot see, it becomes possible to bring God's peace wherever your feet are planted. Experience God's strength and power while wearing His armor, and the powers of darkness set against you will be defeated.

Prayer + Contemplation

01 ———————— Read Ephesians 6:1-12. How might acknowledging that Jesus is always interceding on your behalf help you in your battles, large or small?

02 ———————— Ask the Holy Spirit to help you recognize the devil's schemes and to provide a fresh understanding of how God's weapons of warfare are wielded to defeat the enemy.

03 ———————— Pray for the global church to have a deeper revelation of, and to surrender to the protection of God's armor and the power of His weapons.

Notes + Reflection

_____

_____

_____

_____

Day — 18
Praying for discernment and revelation

The way to know the will of God is to know God and to be rooted in Him.

Today's Scripture

"These are the things God has revealed to us by His Spirit. The Spirit searches all things, even the deep things of God. For who knows a person's thoughts except their own spirit within them? In the same way no one knows the thoughts of God except the Spirit of God. What we have received is not the spirit of the world, but the Spirit who is from God, so that we may understand what God has freely given us."
—1 Corinthians 2:10-12 (NIV)

"I am your servant; give me discernment that I may understand your statutes."
—Psalm 119:125 (NIV)

Reflect on the Word

This world can appear dark, lonely and fearful. We long for the light and beauty of eternity God is preparing for us. Imagine this world as a womb. When a baby is connected through the umbilical cord to their mother, it is nourished, receiving all it needs to grow healthy. When we are connected to God, being "rooted" in Him (Col. 2:7), we have all we need to grow in health.

Hear God's voice saying: "You are never alone in the dark womb of this world. Stay connected to Me, and you will receive all you need to grow fully in Me. Listen, and you will know My voice. Once you grow into all you are created to become, you will be birthed into My presence, seeing Me face to face, where there will no longer be any barriers between us."

He is speaking—do you hear it? We will grow increasingly in His discernment and revelation as we attune our ears to hear and surrender in obedience to Him.

Prayer + Contemplation

01 ———— Read 1 Corinthians 2:6-12. He will reveal all He has prepared for you, as you love, seek and follow God.

02 ———— His Spirit beckons; do you hear it? Pray the words of Psalm 119:125 over your own life, and keep your ears attuned to hear Him.

03 ———— Ask God for His church to increasingly hear His voice and obey, so we can be and do all He created for us.

Notes + Reflection

_____

_____

_____

_____

_____

_____

Empowered *and* sent

Every nation and generation, our own families and neighbors, all need to hear the Good News of what God has done for us in Christ. That cannot happen by our human strength or methodology; only the Spirit's ability to draw people to Jesus can soften hearts to turn from sin and receive the free gift of salvation. As believers, we have a message to proclaim and live.

Day — 19

Power to be witnesses for Jesus

God has promised His Holy Spirit power to those willing to share the Good News with the people He's put in their lives.

Today's Scripture

"But you shall receive power when the Holy Spirit has come upon you; and you shall be witnesses to Me in Jerusalem, and in all Judea and Samaria, and to the end of the earth."
—Acts 1:8 (NKJV)

"And the Spirit and the bride say, 'Come!' And let him who hears say, 'Come!' And let him who thirsts come. Whoever desires, let him take the water of life freely."
—Revelation 22:17 (NKJV)

Reflect on the Word

For many of us, the idea of sharing our faith can often make us nervous and shy. But God promises to give us supernatural power to be His witnesses, across the street and around the world. Isn't it a relief we don't need to rely on our own strength?

Instead, we rely on the Holy Spirit to give us the boldness we need at just the right time and in just the right context. Although we don't know if our words will be received, being an empowered witness for Christ is not determined by our preconceived idea of a successful outcome.

We are called and promised to be empowered to share the Good News of how Jesus is moving in our lives, and how He can do the same in the lives of others.

When the Holy Spirit stirs in you to share about the miraculous power of God, get ready to also be filled with supernatural boldness. It's exciting to join in on the work the Holy Spirit is already doing!

Prayer + Contemplation

01 ——— Ask God to fill you afresh with His power today, to overcome fear and embolden you to be a witness of the Good News of Jesus.

02 ——— Pray for those in your own unique world who are far from God, and ask God to give you the words to say.

03 ——— Pray for those who are called to the ends of the earth as witnesses, that God would give them opportunity, favor and safety.

Notes + Reflection

_____

_____

_____

_____

Day — 20

Power to preach + demonstrate the Gospel

Before we ever open our mouths to preach God's Word, our actions tell a story to those who would hear the Good News.

Today's Scripture

"Because our gospel came to you not simply with words but also with power, with the Holy Spirit and deep conviction. You know how we lived among you for your sake."
—1 Thessalonians 1:5 (NIV)

"Pray also for me, that whenever I speak, words may be given me so that I will fearlessly make known the mystery of the gospel, for which I am an ambassador in chains. Pray that I may declare it fearlessly, as I should."
—Ephesians 6:19-20 (NIV)

Reflect on the Word

There's an oft-quoted exhortation: "Preach the gospel at all times, and if necessary, use words."

Words play a necessary role in sharing the gospel with others, but actions often speak louder than words. Therefore, our lives ought to reflect the truth of the transformational power of Christ to save, change, mobilize and empower us.

Paul's words to the Christ-followers in Thessalonica echo this sentiment. The Holy Spirit can empower our words and deeds to work in unison, to proclaim the gospel. And more so, the Holy Spirit goes before us, preparing hearts to see, hear and receive the Good News.

We are simply messengers, called and empowered to share, with the words God gives us, the work He's doing in our lives and the good deeds He calls us to do.

Prayer + Contemplation

01 ———— How do you see your words and deeds working in unison to proclaim the Good News to the people He's placed in your life?

02 ———— Pray the Lord would bring to mind an area where your words and actions can more closely align with the gospel. Ask Him to help you.

03 ———— Ask the Lord to remove any fear you have of proclaiming the Good News, and to fill you with strength, boldness and fresh joy at His overwhelming goodness.

Notes + Reflection

_____

_____

_____

_____

_____

Power to live in the fullness of God's love

As we wrap up 21 Days of Prayer + Fasting, may you go out into the world to share the gospel, feeling His love all around you.

Today's Scripture

"I pray that out of His glorious riches He may strengthen you with power through His Spirit in your inner being, so that Christ may dwell in your hearts through faith. And I pray that you, being rooted and established in love, may have power, together with all the Lord's holy people, to grasp how wide and long and high and deep is the love of Christ, and to know this love that surpasses knowledge—that you may be filled to the measure of all the fullness of God."
—Ephesians 3:16-19 (NIV)

Additional Scripture

—John 13:34-35 (NLT)

Reflect on the Word

"Ministry and following Jesus don't always have to be hard," a pastor said recently. They weren't suggesting the life lived in Christ is never going to be challenging—that's foolish thinking.

Instead, they meant that Christ's love is so massive that, if we allow it, He will overwhelm us with the glory and grandeur of His love. That love will fill our hearts with a joy that can only come from the indwelling Holy Spirit, revealing Himself and His goodness to us in ever-increasing ways.

On this final day of our 21 Days of Prayer + Fasting, let's consider the driving force of our very existence: the never-ending, overwhelming love of God. May that love define our lives in a new way in the season ahead, wherever the Lord takes us. May it fill every word, every action, every thought—both about ourselves and the world around us. May we live, in every moment, in a constantly growing understanding of the love of God, manifest in the person and work of Jesus.

Prayer + Contemplation

01 ——— Consider Paul's assertion in Ephesians that we may be "filled to the measure of the fullness of God." What might that feel like?

02 ——— Pray that the Lord would fill you afresh with His Spirit and reveal to you in a new way the depth of His love for you.

03 ——— Ask the Lord, as He reveals His love for you in increasing measure, to empower you to love others in greater, more Christlike ways.

Notes + Reflection

_____

_____

_____

_____

_____

A word of thanks

**Thank you for joining us for
21 Days of Prayer + Fasting 2025.**

Our prayer is that you have grown closer to the

Lord and hold a better understanding of the power of the Holy Spirit. Most of all we pray that you know how much you are loved.

A special thanks goes out to everyone who worked on and prayed over this devotional. We hope the last 21 days have been a blessing, and that your family will continue together in prayer and fellowship.

21 Days of Prayer + Fasting 2025 Team

Editors
Marcia Graham
Amanda Borowski
Bill Shepson

Content + Project Coordination
Erin Edquist
Jordan McKenna
Ashleigh Rich

Spanish Translation + Coordination
Diana Edwards
Raul Irigoyen
Rebekka Otremba
Melisa Prieto

Photography, Design + Video
Joshua Hernandez
Caique Morais
PJ Moon

Website
Ben Gurrad

Social Media
Luke La Vine

Special thanks to our writers + contributors:
Daniel A. Brown, Ph.D.; Molly DuQue; John Fehlen;
Timmy Hensel; Melinda Kinsman; Heidi Messner;
Randy Remington; Steve Schell; Jerry Stott, Ph.D.;
Nakisha Wenzel; Andrew Williams, Ph.D.;
Lindsay Willis

21 Days of Prayer+Fasting 2025

Reflect

What did God teach you through these 21 Days of intentional prayer and fasting?

What's next?

You've spent 21 days of Spirit-filled prayer. How might the Holy Spirit be leading you to respond?

Review your reflection notes from the previous page. Now, set your intention for 2025.

21 Days of Prayer + Fasting 2025

Spirit-*Filled* Prayer